Broken_echo

Traces of what used to be...

Dr Pratiksha

BookLeaf
Publishing

India | USA | UK

Dedication

To the version of me who loved without limits,
who stayed too long, hoping love would feel like home.
To the girl who was silenced, shamed, and still kept
choosing love.
This is for her.
And for every soul who gave their all and was left empty.
May you find your voice, your strength, and your way
back to yourself.
You were never too much.
You were just too real for someone not ready.

— Dr Pratiksha

Preface

This book is a collection of wounds—stitched together
with words.

Each poem was born from silence I once swallowed,
from nights I couldn't sleep, from truths I didn't say out
loud.
It carries the ache of betrayal, the weight of letting go,
and the quiet power of rising again.

I did not write these for revenge, pity, or validation.
I wrote them because I owed myself closure.
Because my healing deserved a voice.

If you find yourself somewhere in these pages—hurting,
healing, or halfway through—
Know this: you are not alone.
You are allowed to break, to rebuild, and to begin again.

This isn't just poetry.
It's survival.
It's becoming.

Acknowledgements

To every woman who ever doubted her worth,
questioned her sanity, or held herself together in pieces—
This is for you.

To the ones who left, and to the ones who stayed just
long enough to teach me something—
Your absence gave me space. Your presence gave me
pain. Both gave me poetry.

And to the ones reading this—
May you find in these pages the strength to rise, and the
permission to choose yourself.

1. All in

I was all in—
No doubts, no second thoughts, just trust in the spine.
Wanted to dive deep,
No left, no right, just promises to keep.

How could love arrive so late in my lane,
When he was the only one—why didn't it remain?

I ask you—
What does it take to be someone's one?
I ask you—
What does it take to make two breaths run as one?

Attempt after attempt, my heart on display,
Yet somehow, I was never enough to stay.
The irony bites, cuts sharp, cuts fine—
Even love couldn't get me in line.

2. Untitled (so far)

There were nights I whispered to you,
that just touching your skin wasn't enough.
That 'I love you' felt too small for what I carried inside.
I wanted more of you—more than words,
more than breath, more than time itself.

But how could I ever shape it into language, Wave?
You, whom I named after the ocean,
yet drifted away like a tide that never turned back...

3. Bare souls

Bare souls
Intimate touch
My breath—he'd catch

Want to just merge in him
Want to breathe beneath his skin

Fire burning inside the heart
I thought this love would never part

The way we enclosed each other—
It's what love came to uncover

A blaze ignites between our chests,
Hearts raging—no time, no rest

Steaming through my mind and soul
It's us—none else, just whole

This energy transcends all space

We're not here, just some other place

Become one
Gasp some

We are now JUST one

4. Shaolin

5

We were sitting in a quieter room,
Laughter floating, soft perfume.
I asked you to pour the peg—we were in flow,
Playful hearts, in a golden glow.

I teased, "Oye Kohli, Koli!" with a grin,
Anushka-style, let the games begin.
But you slipped into Instagram's scrollin'—
Lost in the world they call "Shaolin."

A moment of peace, your charm so bright,
I wished for forever, in that Mussoorie night.

I laughed again, "Oye Kohli, peg bana chal, peg bana
naa!"
You made that face—as if it was shaam ka kaam.
The night grew still, stars shy and holy,
Mussoorie sighed, all gamy and dolly.

A memory so small, yet vivid and true—
A flicker of us in a world we once knew.

6

5. Empathy is a curse so deep

Empathy—a curse so deep,
his suffering made my own heart weep.

I wished to take his pain away,
but lost myself along the way.

I wondered how he could survive,
yet in return, was crushed alive.

No, no, no—I dared to dream,
that he would guard my heart, it seemed.

But all I got was lies and pain,
a love that left me lost again.

Marriage was meant to last
I lost myself all so fast

Sorry - "empathy is a curse so deep"

6. last glance of him

I saw you yesterday after days,
For the first time, I felt this way.

You turned my thrill into despair,
My love now floats in empty air.

Once, a glance was all I'd crave,
Now, nothing's left for me to save.

No remorse, no tears to shed,
Just silence where my heart once bled.

They said that marriage isn't a game,
Yet you played it, all the same

7. Flicker

9

I'm shaking, my sight's unclear,
Head feels light, hands shake with fear.
Like my bones have lost their might,
Drifting far from what feels right.

I hold my pup, she warms my chest,
A fleeting hope, a moment's rest.
Was breaking me the price to pay,
For brighter dawns to light my way?

8. Anchor

Long drives, sleepless nights,
Chasing peace with all my might.

Thinking what? I can't define,
Lost in thoughts I can't untwine.

Focus fades, the present slips,
Drifting through the day's eclipse.

Dizziness creeps, my skin turns pale,
Yet my will must rise and sail.

Hope's the light that keeps me sane,
Faith in God, a bond unchained.
I will get through—though times are wild,
I believe, for He's alive.

9. Where our love will survive

Nights grow darker,
Dawn drifts farther.

Life feels withered,
The future—hazy, blurred.

Unbathed for days,
Draped in crinkled haze.

My soul aches,
My efforts weep.

May we meet in the afterlife,
Where our love will survive.

To live in joy, side by side,
Forever there, with no need to hide.

10. Where only dead survives

This story remains untold
My faith is unsold

It took everything for me to built
And a snap for you to kill

Flowers are cold
There is nothing for me to hold

Every single article speak its story here
Even a folded rug weeps tear

Amazon brings the pot
You broke our tied knot

Now dust is all around
Speaks its truth up loud

Love was once where alive
Now only dead survives

13

11. He left me with bundle of memories

He left me with bundle of memories,

That Valentine's night, as you stood in line, lost in
thought,
I slipped away, found a rose, and held it close.

Surprisingly, I placed it in your hand—
a quiet whisper , no demand.

Between the noises i softly gave—
A gesture so small- "i love you wave"

12. Rising through the waves

Waves of sadness hit sometimes,
I say no word, I see no sunshine.

Life is moving, carrying me along,
I'm seeing a new world, trying to be strong.

Pretending to be happy, pretending I'm fine,
My joy dipped far below a nine.

Devastated, destroyed—I've grieved through time,
But life is what it is, and now—I rise, I climb.

13. Tagged and taken - my home

It's the day—
The day when even a single article got separated.
Everything—price-tagged.
At home.
Once what was a home,
Now just a house bygone

What was once emotion,
Is now just an item.
A memory... for sale.
Still, I feel the cuts inside my soul.
My heart still aches.

It's now just a memory I can't even keep.
My heart still longs—
But my mind knows:
It isn't mine to keep.

That flask,

That chopping board,
Even the knife—
They speak their stories here,
But none of them are mine now.
None of them for me to keep.

14. Still "levitating" in memory

It was a family tree—
I was your wife,
You were my "hubban" my world , my glee

Coffee cafés, weekends away,
Parties at night,
Binge-watching YouTube all day.

Hugs and walks,
Kisses and talks.
Seltos on long roads— say
"Levitating" loud on display.

You drove, I danced,
We sang—by chance.

N-H brought us peace,
You'd feast on all the cheese.

At last, we'd hit the bed,
So tired, so unafraid.

We'd fall asleep...
Then Monday came—and we'd weep.

15. This is my side of story

If you're reading this—don't smile.
I bled for every line.

The castle you built stood on shaky land—
And you knew it was destined to END.

Red flags waved, gaslights BURNED,
Yet you held me close—like love was earned.

You turned the table, side by side,
But truth was mine—alone, I cried.

"Nothing" was something you always said,
While lies were the bricks, and silence—the bed.

No one stood when the world took your side,
I trembled, I broke—but clarity survived.

You pointed fingers, threw each blame,
Tried to crush my soul, my name.

"Maniac," "infidel"—your arrows were sharp,
But they pierced my peace, left me in the dark.

I cried till blood oozed from inside—
No wound untouched, no place to hide.

That's when I chose to rise,
To learn, to say goodbyes

I pushed myself aside for love—
Now I rise above.

16. I now picked up the pen

I loved a shadow, not a man—
Just a mask that knew how to stand.

You printed bruises deep inside—
That's when I chose to step aside.

You tried to script both start and end,
But this time, I picked up the pen.

There are still things my silence holds,
Still echoes - no ear ever told.

Now, when I look back from the door,
I feel more fierce, more free than before.

No regrets—nothing to possess.
I chose me, and revoked your access.

With quiet fire, I now ascend—
Determined, I move the wind's direction instead.

17. Not a tale of blame

23

You said—"I didn't save this relationship after the fight"
I say—I only stayed when nothing felt right.

Tried to hold love that slipped like sand,
While you just watched with folded hands.

Still, I rose, piece by piece,
Found my calm, chose my peace.

This is not a tale of blame—
It's the end - i'm done with your game

18. An apology

An apology I deserve — from me, to me
I never made myself feel this terribly.

For overthinking, for forgetting my worth,
For breaking down, for staying through the hurt.

I recited — "If a wife isn't happy in marriage, she
becomes strong,"
But strength shouldn't mean suffering all along.

I owe myself soft mornings and peace at night,
Not walking on eggshells or dimming my light.

So here's my sorry — wrapped in truth and grace,
I forgive the girl who stayed in that place.

She did her best with all she knew,
But now, she walks in something new.

19. I choose me : finally

I was once hoping for more,
Standing still outside your door.

For love, for care, for validation—
All I met was quiet betrayal, and hesitation.

Just once, I wished you'd feel me for me,
Just once, you'd simply let me be.

But once hoping—now no more,
I've turned and walked from that old door.

Now and forever, I choose me for me,
Now and forever, I let it all be.

20. A mirror- YOU now

I want to sincerely thank you,
For the pain you gave—I grew

'Control'—wrapped in the name of 'protection',
I mistook it for love, but it was your obsession.

The exit you gave
Turned into my freedom wave.

You thought I wouldn't survive—
But look at me now... I thrive.

You said, "You're digging your own grave."
Remember this—I was always brave.

I told you once—I'm a mirror, and now you see how.
So take this truth: Don't play with fire now.

21. Wiggle's right beneath my chest

Uff..!
This wiggle sits right beneath my chest,
It aches so bad when I revisit the rest—
My past, my choice, that one decision,
How did I not see through your precision?

How could you pretend what never was?
Tie it with vows, wrap it in gauze.
Marriage—a promise meant to be kept,
You walked away with a sigh, while I wept.

Like it was nothing—just playful, just art,
Then came your weeping—such a dramatic part.
You spoke of how bold you'd always been,
You vented loud—but God has seen.

Oh yes—He's seen your careful disguise,
Your game of victim, your clever lies.
Respect—was that too much to ask?

Why did you hide behind a hollow mask?

I can't explain how you drained my worth,
But now you're gone... I breathe on this earth.
I fly—unchained, chaos-free,
No more knots tying down me.

You were just a lesson burned,
Yet through the ashes—I still learned.
I still believe in love you scorched,
But hope—my fire—you never torched.

Hope is fire, I kept it alive,
Because without it—how does one survive?

22. Healing without hate

I'm not weak for feeling this deep,
For wounds that ache and thoughts that creep.
I loved, I hoped, I dreamed, I tried—
But something tender in me died.

I don't wish harm, I'm not that flame,
But I won't wear the weight of shame.
I seek no vengeance, no cruel reply,
Just peace beneath an honest sky.

I want my space, my breath, my ground,
Where healing speaks without a sound.
I'll walk away with grace, not spite—
But I won't hush my inner light.

So hear this truth, both fierce and kind:
I won't betray my heart or mind.
I'll let him go without regret—
But I won't forget myself again.

23. Closure isn't always a conversation

Closure Isn't Always a Conversation
Sometimes, it's quiet self-preservation.

No call, no text, no final say—
Just choose yourself and walk away.

You cry once, and never again.
Your heart will heal through your own pen.

You learn the truth without confession,
Love yourself—no need for permission.

So no, I don't need you. No "sorry."
I found my freedom, in my own story.

It's not the end—
It's where you begin..